HAPPINESS

POEMS OF
LIFE AND LOVE

KATHRYN CAROLE ELLISON

Published by Lady Bug Books, an imprint of Brisance Books Group.
Lady Bug Press and the distinctive ladybug logo are registered trademarks of
Lady Bug Books, LLC.

Lady Bug Books
400 112th Avenue N.E.
Suite 230
Bellevue, WA 98004
www.GiftsOfLove.com

For information about custom editions, special sales and permissions, please email
Info@GiftsOfLove.com

Manufactured in the United States of America
ISBN: 978-1-944194-94-9

First Edition: November 2023

A note from the author

The poems in this book were written over many years as gifts to my children. I began writing them in the 1970s, when they were reaching the age of reason. As I found myself in the position of becoming a single parent, I wanted to do something special to share with them – something that would become a tradition, a ritual they could count on.

And so the Advent Poems began – one day, decades ago – with a poem 'gifted' to them each day during the Advent period leading up to Christmas, December 1 to December 24. Nearly fifty years later, my kids still look forward each year to the 'gifted' poems that continue a family tradition, and that new generations have come to cherish.

It is my sincere hope that you will embrace and enjoy them and share them with those you love.

Children of the Light was among the early poems I wrote, and is included in each of the *Poems of Life and Love* books in The Ellison Collection: (alphabetically) *Awakenings, Beginnings, Celebrations, Choices, Conversations, Gratitude, Happiness, Heartstrings, Horizons, Inspirations, Milestones, Mindfulness, Moments, Possibilities, Reflections, Sanctuary, Sojourns,* and *Tapestry.*

After writing many hundreds of poems, *Children of the Light* is still my favorite. In the process of writing it, the words seemed to spring from my heart, and soul... and flowed so effortlessly that it was written in a single sitting. All I needed to do was capture the words on paper.

"Light," to me represents all that is good and pure and right with the world, and I believed then – as I do today – that those elements live in my children, and in all of us.

We need only to dare.

– KCE

DEDICATION

To My Parents: Herb and Bernice Haas

Mom, you were the poet who went before me.
Thanks for paving the way.
From you I learned to appreciate the power of Poetry.

And Dad (Daddy), you always believed in me,
no matter what direction my life took.
Thank you for your faith in me,
and for your unconditional love.

TABLE OF CONTENTS

LIFE'S JOYS

LIFE'S LESSONS

Life's gifts

LIFE'S JOYS

HAPPINESS

"Some people cause happiness wherever they go,
And others..." when they leave the scene.
Oscar Wilde, with biting wit, shared this thought.
Was he humorously venting his spleen?

Happiness doesn't depend on external conditions.
It is governed by your mental attitude.
You can find it with others, crowds large and small;
And you can find it when you're in complete solitude.

Happiness is inward, and not outward;
It depends not on what you possess.
Instead, it depends on what you are
As you continue along in your process.

Happiness is a direction, not a place.
Your lives will continue to unfold.
As only a moving bicycle can remain in balance
You must keep moving, and sharing happiness, I am told.

THE PURE OF HEART

Look out with love from your pure heart
And feel the warmth which radiates
Back in, and circles round your soul.
Giving love reciprocates.

Your behavior invites like conduct.
You get back what you give out.
To others you must instruct
The good that you are about.

The freedom lies within your soul
To act with love, respect and peace.
Your personhood shines pure and whole.
Heart actions cause your struggles to cease.

LAUGHTER

Laughter has been called an instant vacation...
It is sunshine in the house... it has no foreign accent.
It's the shortest distance between two people;
That it makes you feel happy is no accident.

When you laugh, your body produces endorphins –
Hormones which relieve your pain and your stress...
Endorphin release gives you a natural ˈhigh...ˈ
A feeling of well-being and hopefulness.

Socrates said, ˈThe Comic and the Tragic
Lie inseparably close, like light and shadow.ˈ
We are constantly comparing one to the other,
And pondering what reaction might be apropos.

George Bernard Shaw confirmed this premise...
In fact, it could even be his monograph:
ˈLife doesn't cease to be funny when people die
Any more than it ceases to be serious when people laugh.ˈ

It's said that an optimist laughs to forget
While a pessimist forgets to laugh at all.
e.e. Cummings said, "The most wasted of all days
Is one without laughter" – morning to nightfall.

"A good laugh heals a lot of hurts."
So says Madeleine L'Engle – so wise.
Mark Twain: "Against the assault of laughter,
Nothing can stand" – no need to analyze.
Lord Byron quoted: "Always laugh when you can!
It's cheap medicine." – it's true, I realize.
Erma Bombeck said, "When humor goes,
There goes civilization!" – a need to dramatize.

Laughing is always the best form of therapy,
It's the opposite of being sad and downcast.
Laughter is mankind's most effective weapon.
As Mary Poole stated: "He who laughs, lasts!"

A SENSE OF WONDER

Socrates stated, and it was recorded:
"Wondering is the beginning of wisdom..." at hand.
Wonder is brought about by experiencing mystery;
It's the basis of humans' desire to understand.

Through the beauty of nature you are led to wonder "why."
Charlie Chaplin put it so simply when this he shared:
"You'll never find a rainbow if you're always looking down."
The wonder-ful is all around you. Sometimes you're unprepared.

The magic doesn't end because you've figured out
How something works that once was so mysterious.
The wonder lasts... you've gained new knowledge.
The joy of expanding knowledge can make you delirious.

The feeling of awed wonder that science can give us
Is one of the highest experiences in the world.
It may not happen often, but when it does,
It's as if the answer was waiting to be unfurled.

REST

There is virtue in work, and there is virtue in rest.
Balance between the two is the key to a happier lifestyle.
You've given a hundred percent effort to the job at hand;
You've earned the peace of mind, you've gone the extra mile.

Withdraw from the cares that won't withdraw from you.
Press "pause" to let everything sink in.
Rest is not idleness, you must rest when you're weary;
Then you're back to work refreshed, with new energy to begin.

Your calm mind is the ultimate weapon against stress…
Stress from challenges, both professional and personal.
Slow down and enjoy life and plan where you're going—
Relaxation is the answer – and remember, stress is optional.

Lying on the grass under trees on a summer's day
And watching clouds as they drift across the sky
Is not a waste of time, by any means.
Rest refreshes your soul. Your energy will multiply.

POSITIVE ENERGY

Let's face it – you attract the energy you give off!
It comes back to you, sometimes tenfold!
It would make good sense then, would it not,
To send positive vibes; let positive energy take hold.

You'll see that replacing negative thoughts
With positive ones will make a difference.
With no ˮenemyˮ lurking inside of you,
Any ˮenemyˮ outside doesn't stand a chance!

You give life to what you give energy to;
Generate positive energy in all of your doings.
It's contagious, and others will pass it on.
All humanity benefits, as joy you are pursuing.

We like to be around those who are joyful—
Who emit positive energy at every turn.
Positive thoughts, words and actions create positive feelings...
Which generate positive energy, you will learn.

GRATITUDE

A grateful heart is a magnet for miracles…
You shift to a higher frequency and attract better things.
You give joy and laughter to all those around you.
Communication occurs along loving heartstrings.

With gratitude in your heart there's more beauty to see.
Opening your eyes enhances your gratitude practice.
Be thankful for everything that happens in your life…
It is all your experience! It's your very own process.

Gratitude is when memory is stored in your heart,
And not in your busy mind at all.
An "attitude of gratitude" will ease your path.
It will help you survive any storm or squall.

There'll be moments, of course, when your gratitude wears thin,
And it's rekindled by another on the spot.
They've lit the flame within you to go another turn.
Be grateful when things are going well. Be graceful when they are not.

PEACE ON EARTH

It's said that peace begins with a smile,
And it comes from within; don't seek it from without.
The behavior of others can test the measure
Of the inner peace you carry through the fallout.

"Peace cannot be kept by force."
(This... according to Einstein)
"It can only be achieved by understanding."
Peace comes through you; that's the bottom line.

You have peace when you make it with yourself.
And peace is a day-by-day process.
Opinions gradually change; old barriers slowly erode.
With practice, it can become effortless.

"Do your little bits of good where you are..."
(As Desmond Tutu so wisely shared)
"Put them together – they can overwhelm the world."
It's an important way to show that you cared.

Someone asked me once when my "justice mode" was flaring,
"Do you want to be happy or right?"
Happy is peaceful, keeping stillness inside,
While winning at being right requires a fight.

When the power of love replaces the love of power
Then world peace will be given a chance.
Peace is not God's gift to his creatures...
Peace is our gift to each other – do the dance!

CHERISH EVERY MOMENT

Mother Teresa tells us to "be happy in the moment."
That moment is the only one about which we have choice.
The past is past; the future's not yet here.
It's always the now... we can cry or rejoice.

Today is life... the only life you're sure of.
Don't spoil it by wishing you'd done something better...
And don't spend it wondering what you're going to do next.
"Be Here Now" is your mantra. I'm sure you concur.

If you spend your life waiting for the storm,
You'll never enjoy the sunshine in the skies.
Stay in the moment; look for the beauty around you.
It's there for the viewing. Open your eyes.

Get everything you can from each day you're alive.
Soak it up and cherish each experience.
Each day is a piece of the mosaic of your life.
Live fully each day in the "present tense."

THINKING POSITIVELY

"As a man thinketh so he is,"
Was said in wisdom long ago.
So it would follow, would it not,
That thinking "positive" is the way to go?

We tend to become exactly the person
The thoughts in our head prepare us to be.
To find greater peace and happiness here,
The first step is thinking positively.

IT'S A NEW DAY

Today is the perfect day for a new beginning.
Really, there's no better time than now!
You're always in charge of your thoughts about your life;
It's up to you to determine the why and the how.

Just one small positive thought in the morning
Can change how your day will play itself out.
Each day holds the possibility of your rebirth.
Pursue it with positivity, deleting all doubt.

Think of it as an investment, an investment in you...
One small step towards happiness and good cheer.
So what will you do today, here and now,
That will make you proud of yourself in a year?

If change is the goal you are seeking for yourself –
A change in the manner your life unfolds –
Then the choices you've made must be revisited
And new choices put in place; lose the old!

Every morning starts a new page in your story.
You have responsibility to make the narrative sing!
Drop the broken pieces of the past. They're behind you.
Make each moment count, and enjoy the upswing.

Treat each new dawn of each new day
As special as it deserves to be treated.
Think of the New Year, and the attention it receives,
Then apply it daily! It is to be repeated.

OPTIMISM

"Take short views, hope for the best, and
Believe in God," said a Smith named Syd.
He lived in the past, but his words live on.
He must have been quite a kid!

The "hope for the best" part of his line
Is the one in focus right here.
Optimism about everything we see and do
Is the way to remove any fear.

Approach everything and everyone
With love... not fear or negative thought.
The results will most often be in line
With the attitude which you have brought.

The earth is turning, the sun is shining!
You are alive! Celebrate the now!
Look forward with joy to what will come.
Your thoughts will start with, "Wow!"

Your impact on others is positive and good.
You are a powerful personality, you're strong!
You exude optimism and strength to all.
You help others learn to sing their own song.

FRIENDSHIP

It's said that friends are the family you choose,
Whether they're actually related to you or not.
Aristotle answers the question: "What is a friend?
A single soul dwelling in two bodies." (That's a lot!)

Friendship is the hardest thing in the world to explain.
It's not something you learn in school.
It can take time, or happen at the drop of a hat;
And, true friendship lasts, as a rule.

"The glory of friendship is when you discover
That someone believes in you... and is willing
To trust you with friendship..." according to Emerson.
A modest name for the feeling is "fulfilling."

Friendship is built on respect and trust.
Both elements have to be mutually there.
You can respect someone, but if trust isn't present
The friendship will crumble beyond repair.

No person is your friend who demands your silence,
Or denies your right to grow.
Your best friends are those who bring out your best.
Make those friends always part of your "show."

Surrender

Always say "yes" to the present moment.
It's futile to resist what already is.
It would be insane to oppose life itself,
Which is now, it's now. Now it is.

Surrender to what is; say "yes" to life,
And be amazed at the results that come next.
Life suddenly starts working for, not against, you.
Let the world embrace you, don't be perplexed.

Amazing things happen when you surrender, and simply love;
You melt into the power already within you.
The world changes when you change, and softens when you soften.
The world loves you when you decide to love it, too.

Be willing to let go of the life that you have,
So you can have the life that is waiting in the wings.
If you surrender completely to each present moment,
You'll live more richly as human beings.

LIFE'S LESSONS

RESILIENCE

"The greatest glory in living lies not in never falling,
But in rising every time we fall."
Nelson Mandela uttered these words of wisdom.
He suffered many hardships, after all.

No matter how many burdens fall on you,
Keep on moving... keep plowing ahead.
You are not a product of what's happened before.
You have the power of choice; be positive, instead.

Life doesn't get easier, or more tolerant...
You get stronger and more resilient.
What hurt you in the past can help you face the present.
The goal is to thrive... move forward with good intent.

What helps you persevere is your resilience and commitment...
That... and an attitude of forgiving.
Holding grudges weighs you down, and holds you back.
Falling down is part of life; getting back up is living.

FEAR OF FAILURE

What would you attempt to do
If you knew you could not fail?
If all restraints were taken away
How high would you dare to scale?

If all your needs were met and you
Were free to follow your dream,
How far would you go, and what would you do?
Just what would be your theme?

The fear we place on failure can be
What holds us back from glory.
We worry what others might think of us –
We heed the "derogatory."

So... failure is but an attitude, and
It doesn't exist at all.
No matter how high you choose to climb,
It's impossible for you to fall.

PATIENCE

Consider the subject of patience, will you?
How do you suppose it can be demonstrated?
Patience is to remain calm in any situation,
No matter how much you are aggravated.

Patience forces you to pay attention.
It's important to gain facts before you act.
Patience is a calm acceptance that things might happen
In a time frame not of your choosing... inexact.

Patience is the direct antithesis of anger.
Nature never rushes, yet everything gets done.
It is well to remember that things take time.
Patience and time can do more than strength or passion.

It does seem strange that the years teach us patience.
The shorter time we have left, the more comfortable the wait.
Perhaps experience... years of it... has taught us
That things happen in their own time, and we celebrate.

DYNAMIC LIVING

Let everything you do
Be dynamic to your awareness;
Let it matter most to you;
Let it add to your "being–there–ness."

To live as if a robot...
To live automatically
Is slipping back a step...
I mean, "evolutionarily."

To know and then to act
As if you're in denial
Is not being true to you,
And it really lacks in style.

So be aware of every part
Of your life, without and within.
Be an observer **and** a participant
And you'll be sure to "win."

Believe in yourself

No matter the number of kudos you receive –
All well-earned, that goes without saying –
The final and, by far, most important hurrah
Is that one to yourself you are paying.

Believe in yourself, believe in the good
You generate wherever you go.
Your capacity for goodness is greater, by far,
Than any measure you can know.

All will be well if you but believe
In your own potential for good.
Your actions reflect your picture of yourself;
You automatically do as you should.

(This "should" is not an external law,
Ruling your behavior from outside.
It's one you hold to be true at your core.
It allows you to select, with pride.)

Your acceptance of self, and your ability to share
Your good feelings along your life's course
Are the keys to your victories, your map to the stars.
Stay in touch with your own life source.

SEEKING HAPPINESS

Is happiness what you seek above all else?
Is it the goal you pursue every waking hour?
If you're not feeling happy, is it someone else's fault?
(I can't believe you give someone else that much power.)

A lifelong search, if that's your style,
To go chasing after happiness all over the land?
Happiness is like a cloud that evaporates in time...
It's a by-product – not a thing to hold in your hand.

Herman Hesse explained happiness another way:
"Happiness is a 'how,' not a 'what.'"
...it's "a talent, not an object," he continued to say.
From another perspective, it cannot be bought.

"We can only be happy now," it is said,
"And there will never be a time when it is not now."
Gerald Jampolsky shared this wisdom with us.
(He clears up some questions about time, somehow.)

"Be happy for this moment. This moment is your life."
Omar Khayyam is credited with this thought.
Happiness is a by-product – you cannot touch it or see it.
You can only enjoy it if it is what you've brought.

Describing happiness and how to have it
Is best explained by what it is not.
Happiness is the absence of striving for it!
Stop your desperate search and 'follow the dots.'

The ancients suggested that the chiefest point of happiness
Is that a person is willing to be what he/she is.
Choose to be happy. It is good for your health.
I suggest it strongly (with much emphasis).

You're more apt to find happiness when you help others find theirs.
Do not worry about who's ahead in the score.
To forget oneself is to be happy, it is said,
And the happiest of all are those who give more.

AUTHENTICITY AND ACTION

Be an observer of all behavior
So that you can become more open
To more behavioral possibilities.

You will learn a great deal more
When you are open to everything.
Do not just aim to please the teacher.

Style can never replace what's true,
And simple wisdom holds its own
With knowing all specific facts.

Potency is acting from one's center,
Not from creating an impression of strength,
Even if others are willing to be fooled.

An authentic person who is well centered
Can do the task at hand with ease,
And be effective... not just busy.

Effective action arises out of
Silence and a clear sense of being,
And offers you a source of peace.

WHAT DO YOU HAVE TO LOSE?

Since yesterday is certainly not yours to recover,
You can turn your attention to the moment, and plan.
Tomorrow is yours to win or lose,
So aim to win; don't be an "also-ran."

If you win, it's you; if you lose, it's you.
It's black and white; there's nowhere to hide.
It's all about you, and you alone.
Over your life's happenings you must preside.

Winning is great! You're riding high,
And the feeling cannot be beat.
But losing could happen and you'd better be ready
To learn from it, get up, and repeat.

You're not getting any younger, so why the fear
Of following your heart and your mind?
It's a trap to think you have something to lose,
When your efforts should be on something to find.

WALK AWAY FROM THE DRAMA

There should come a time in everyone's life
When being caught up in other people's theater
Becomes a burden he or she need not endorse,
And the best thing to do is retreat.

Surround yourself with people who make you laugh.
Love the people who treat you right.
Life's too short to be anything but happy.
Focus on the good with all your might.

Walk away from the drama and the people who create it.
You need not get caught in their snare.
Falling down with trouble is a part of life.
Getting back up is living, with joy to share.

BE IN THE NOW

It's a matter of now, that's all there is —
No past, no future can bow
Into your lives unless you let it.
You're always here and now.

Sometimes it's difficult to remember,
As your mind goes forward or to the past
And scoops up memories or fantasies
(May only the good ones last),
That to dream or recall what might be, or was,
Can sometimes be a dead end
'Cause it can prevent you from enjoying the now
Unless you can always tend
To know the difference between mind play and fact.
It's the sign of a healthy mind.
You have the health. You're quick. You're smart.
And you're ever, ever so kind.

As long as you remember to be
Open and trusting and kind;
And remember the source of life's greatest love,
You'll never get into a bind.
It springs from the heart, it's ever-present;
It molds your way of dealing
With those you know and those you don't.
It's a powerful, wonderful feeling.

BALANCE BETWEEN WORK AND REST

There is virtue in work, and there is virtue in rest.
Balance between the two allows a happier lifestyle.
You've given a hundred percent effort to the job at hand;
You've earned your peace of mind, you've gone the extra mile.

Withdraw from the cares that won't withdraw from you.
Press "pause" to let everything sink in.
Rest is not idleness; you must rest when you're weary,
Then back to work refreshed with new energy to begin.

A calm mind is the ultimate weapon against stress...
Stress from challenges, both professional and personal.
Slow down, enjoy life, and determine where you're going.
Relaxation is the answer; and remember... stress is optional.

Lying on the grass under trees on a summer's day
Or watching clouds as they drift across the sky
Is not a waste of time, by any means.
Rest refreshes your soul; your energy will multiply.

ENTHUSIASM

Enthusiasm moves the world, it has been stated.
It spells the difference between mediocrity and success.
Enthusiasm spawns effort and the power of action.
Passion for what you're doing brings results with cheerfulness.

Enthusiasm is the agitation that makes your hopes shine.
It's the sparkle in your eyes; it's the joy in your giving.
Enthusiasm is not the same as just being excited...
It's your faith in something that makes life worth living.

Protect your enthusiasm from the negativity of others.
Carry a child's spirit with you into old age.
That means not losing the passion for loving life.
Life gives back in kind. You will have an advantage.

Remember this wisdom throughout your life
As you pursue with joy and enthusiasm your goal.
The years pile on; they may wrinkle the skin,
But to give up enthusiasm wrinkles your soul.

CHILDREN OF THE LIGHT

There are those souls who bring the light,
Who spill it out for all to share.
And with a joy that does excite,
They show the world that they do care.
It is so very bright.

In this sharing, love does pervade
Into their lives and cycles round;
And as this light is outward played
The love is also inward bound.
It is an awesome trade.

You are a soul whose light is shared.
It comes from deep within your heart.
It's best because it is not spared,
Because it's total, not just part.
And I am glad you've dared.

GEORGE SANTYANA ON HAPPINESS

Sometimes when we have it
We don't recognize it;
It is our nature to be volatile.
Domestic bliss
Can be right at hand,
And we don't see it, meanwhile.

If happiness is
Domestic bliss
(And surely that definition qualifies),
Then we must be patient
To appreciate
What we have before it flies.

Volatile spirits
Prefer unhappiness;
It's sad, but true, as they say.
So, guard against
Those careless thoughts,
Or happiness can fly away.

QUESTIONS

Very few people really seek knowledge –
They approach the unknown with an agenda,
And try to wring answers they've already shaped
With justifications, confirmations and addenda.

To really ask the question and be open to the answer
Might open the door to a whirlwind of wisdom.
The questions you ask of yourselves will determine
The type of people you will eventually become.

Remember this wisdom regarding your questions:
There will be many of varying importance.
The most important ones in life can't be answered
By anyone except yourself. Do your dance.

It's the questions you can't answer that teach you the most.
They teach you how to think things through.
Given an answer, all you gain is a little fact,
But a question requires the most work by you.

Have patience with what remains unsolved.
Try to love the questions themselves.
Like locked rooms and books in another tongue,
Your search continues for yourselves.

SEE THINGS FOR WHAT THEY ARE

"What you see is what you'll get."
Open your eyes wide enough to see.
Seeing things for what they really are
Takes experience, you must agree.

The truth may not meet with your expectations.
People's behavior and events are out of your control.
Spare yourself the pain of false attachments.
Embrace what you get as you watch it unroll.

When something happens, the only thing in your power
Is your attitude toward it. I know you see.
You can accept it as is; or if not, be resentful.
Accepting seems wiser, you will agree.

LIFE'S GIFTS

VISUALIZATIONS

To be that one who lives up to your dreams...
To catch up with your images and schemes...

To speak as if your goals for self are true...
To enter each stage of life on the right cue...

If plans to reach these goals are interrupted,
Then chances are your thinking is corrupted.

To see yourself as one who doesn't fit
Will keep you there, or in some other pit.

But seeing self in better light requires
Your thinking positively... no more mires.

You do become the person of your thoughts...
You act scenarios, and even plots...

So visualize, my dear. With each dream, savor.
The inner voice works wonders in your favor.

WORK TO LIVE... OR LIVE TO WORK

A regret found mostly with men who were dying
Is that they wished they hadn't worked so hard.
They felt loss of connection with children and wives.
Their lives of work had not reaped the reward.

Simplifying your life and getting off the treadmill,
Where your work dominates every waking hour,
Is a way to take stock and be open to explore
New opportunities where you are happier.

HAPPINESS AND HEALTH

"I have chosen to be happy because it is good for my health!"
Voltaire penned these now-famous words long ago.
It's thought that your body hears everything your mind says —
Make sure your self-talk is positive, as through your life you go.

A healthy outside starts from the inside;
Our thoughts propel us, our bodies follow.
A calm mind brings inner strength and confidence
Which are important for good health, as you know.

Most people have no idea how well their bodies are designed
For feeling good and healthy and alive.
Health is more than the absence of disease.
It's your inner spirit glowing. You are meant to thrive.

People who laugh live longer than those who don't.
The key to a healthy body is having a healthy mind.
What fuels your spirit actually fuels your body.
Happiness and health are forever intertwined.

Happiness can be found, even in the darkest of times
If you can remember to turn on your own light.
Only you can do it... you and you alone.
Find the wick, light your match, and it will ignite.

Start each day with a grateful heart.
Your inner and outer health is your greatest wealth.
The Dalai Lama sums it up with these simple words:
"Happiness is the highest form of health."

ACCEPTANCE

Accepting things as they are may be hard,
But necessary for a life free from pain.
Longfellow said it best, "When it's raining
The best thing to do is let it rain."

Acceptance does not mean resignation,
Nor running away from the fray;
But accepting your life as it comes...
With handicaps and all, by the way.

The handicaps might include many things,
Including what you inherited at birth;
Or suffering the ills of all the world.
There are plenty of them on this earth.

Acceptance of what's happened is always
The first step to overcoming tribulations.
Happiness grows in direct proportion to acceptance,
And in inverse proportion to one's expectations.

Not everything that is faced can be changed
But nothing can be changed until it's faced.
When you accept yourself as you are...
Then, if you wish, change of self can take place.

Alan Watts had words about acceptance:
"To make sense out of change, plunge into it...
Move with that change, and join the dance."
Dance well, my loves, and don't quit.

SELF-CONFIDENCE

If you put a small value upon yourself,
Know that the world will not raise your price.
No, the onus is on you to elevate your value.
Go out and get busy... act now, is my advice.

When you begin to recognize your own worth
It will be hard to be with people who do not.
You'll acquire positive new friends when you're more confident.
Your life will feel like you've hit the jackpot!

Self-confidence is a most attractive quality.
It comes from not fearing to be wrong.
Surround yourself with those who bring out the best in you...
Be curious and full of wonder all your life long.

Believe in yourself; be content with yourself;
Do not strive for approval from any other.
Accept yourself – your self-acceptance matters most.
The whole world will fall in place, one incident after another.

EXCITEMENT

It is said that excitement is a mixture of enthusiasm,
Motivation, intuition and a hint of creativity.
Excitement will lead you through most obstacles,
And enhance your spirits and your productivity.

Be happy with what you have, but be excited about what you want.
Your wings already exist... all you have to do is fly!
Give yourself permission to act like a child...
View the world with wonder; on your dreams you can rely.

Do not worry about the things that might go wrong.
Instead, get excited about all that can go right.
You'll have more fun if you embrace the excitement,
And you'll have a better chance to reach the heights!

"Be in love with your life, every moment of it..."
Jack Kerouac reminds us of its importance.
Share your excitement every day you exist...
It's contagious! You are helping our culture advance.

RELATIONSHIP

A relationship requires work and commitment;
And conflict is bound to come up once in a while.
Then the factor that damages or deepens your friendship
Is your attitude, your willingness to stay awhile.

It's your willingness to see the innocence in others
That allows you to see it (that's my observation).
A person is who they've been throughout your relationship,
Not who they were in your last conversation.

In life you'll realize there's a purpose for everyone
Whom you meet as you travel east or west.
Some will test or use you, and some will teach;
But most importantly, some will bring out your best.

Keep people in your life who love and motivate you.
Make each other happy; it's a mutual benefit.
And find joy in everything you choose to do...
It's your responsibility to love it or change it.

Do not neglect the people most important to you,
Thinking they'll always be available – your ˈregulars.ˈ
Because one day you may wake up and find
You lost the moon while counting the stars.

It is less important to have more friends
Than it is to have fewer who are real.
You be the friend that you want to have;
Seeking the best in others has the most appeal.

The basic thing that holds a relationship together –
The most essential ingredient in communication –
Is trust. That's trust with a capital ˈT.ˈ
That's a fact. That's beyond speculation.

ASPIRATIONS

A synonym for hopes and also for dreams
Is the word "aspirations" – it's all the same theme.
Your visions look outward and become aspirations.
Fulfilling them brings joy and feelings of exaltation.

Your aspirations are always your possibilities,
And a sure thing, when you pursue with your abilities.
Within your aspirations you find your opportunities;
Quite often they show up in your own communities.

People with goals know where they are going;
They aspire to success with ideas free-flowing.
Place your own goals at the top of your checklist,
And pay no attention to any doubts that persist.

Do not lose hold of your dreams or aspirations.
Settling for mediocre is no consolation.
Without dreams you still exist, but without your life force.
Follow your dreams, Loves! Stay the course!

EXERCISE

When we're kids we don't think of making the time
To exercise, to keep our bodies fit.
It's natural to run and play outside.
We don't think about fitness... we "just do it."
Movement is a medicine for creating change –
With physical, emotional, and mental benefit.
The hardest thing about exercise is
Starting to do it, and making it a habit.
But after you start, the hardest thing
Is to stop doing it, I submit.

It is a celebration of what your body can do,
Not a punishment for what you ate.
Fitness is the key to a healthy body
And frees your mood to elevate.
Physical activity is the ultimate stress–buster.
An early morning walk will always rejuvenate.
We do not stop exercising because we grow old...
It's the other way around, there's no debate.
There's a warning to be stated about exercise:
It causes health and happiness, you can appreciate.

HAPPINESS CAN ONLY BE FOUND WITHIN

Freedom is won by disregarding things
That lie beyond our control (an admonition).
Light heartedness and joy cannot enter your mind
When it's busy processing fear and ambition.

Freedom equates happiness – interchangeable points
On the scale of life's choices for existence.
Do not enter into combat with what you have
No control over. It doesn't make sense.

Your happiness depends on only three things,
And all of them are within your power, you see:
Your will; your ideas concerning your situation;
And the use you make of those ideas. That's the key.

Authentic happiness is always independent
Of external conditions in all of their hues.
Your happiness can only be found within.
Practice indifference to the external views.

It's easy to be dazzled by others' trappings –
Celebrity, job title, degrees, wealth or talent.
Don't aspire to be anyone but your own best self,
And happiness is yours. You've found it.

DREAMS

Dreams are not what you experience while sleeping.
No, they're the things that do not let you sleep.
Your dreams are your realities... those in waiting.
Sow the seeds of your future; your realities you shall reap.

Some people think there's not enough time for their dreams;
But, of course, that cannot possibly be true.
If you have a heartbeat, there's time for your dreams,
So dream on and pursue. The onus is on you.

Be fearless in the pursuit of what sets your soul on fire!
Your dreams are given to you for a reason.
What if you fail?... No, but what if you fly?
Your pursuit will continue, no matter the season.

Never mind if it's difficult to follow your dream;
To not follow it would be simply absurd.
Let your dreams be bigger than your fears any day,
And your actions be louder than your words.

A CLOSING THOUGHT

POETRY

It's the revelation
Of a sensation
That the poet
(Wouldn't you know it)
Believes to be
Felt only interiorly
And personal to
The writer who
... writes it.

It's the interpretation
Of a sensation
That was fueled by
A poet's sigh
And believed to be
Shared mutually
And personal to
The lucky one who
... reads it.

About the author

Kathryn Carole Ellison is a former newspaper columnist
and journalist and, of course, a poet.

She lives near her children and stepchildren and their families in the
Pacific Northwest, and spends winters in the sunshine of Arizona.

You might find her on the golf course, traveling the world, writing poems,
or enjoying the arts in the company of dear friends.

Late bloomer

Our culture honors youth with all
It's unbridled effervescence.
We older ones sit back and nod
As if in acquiescence.

And when our confidence really gels
In early convalescence…
"We can't be getting old!" we cry,
"We're still struggling with adolescence!"

Acknowledgments

I have many people to thank...

First of all, my (now) adult children, Jon and Nicole LaFollette, and Jon's wife Eva LaFollette, for inspiring the writing of the poems in the first place... and for encouraging me to continue writing poems, even though their wisdom and understanding, and their compassion, surpasses mine...

And thanks to the rest of my wonderful family that I inherited in 1985 when I married their father, Bill Ellison... Debbie Bacon, Jeff Ellison and Tom Ellison, and their respective spouses, John, Sandy and Sue. They, along with their children and grandchildren, are a major part of my daily living, and I am blessed to have them in my life.

Thank you, good friends, who have received poems of mine in Christmas cards over the years, for complimenting the messages in my poems.

Your encouragement helped to keep me writing and gave me the courage to publish.

I am indebted to Kim Kiyosaki who introduced me to the right person to get the publishing process under way... Mona Gambetta with Brisance Books Group has made the publishing process seem easy. I marvel at her abilities and her good humor, and treasure our friendship.

Thanks to Amy Anderson, Sonya Kopetz, Kerri Kazarba Schneider, and Ingrid Pape-Sheldon, my very first, most creative, public relations team of experts who have helped to carry my poems and my story to the world.

And... finally, thanks to John B. Laughlin, a fellow traveler in life, who encourages me every day in the writing and publishing process.

John, I love having you along for this magical ride.

Books of Life and Love
by Kathryn Carole Ellison